# NEXT STEPS

# Careers in Welding

Andrea Vergun

NEXT STEPS Careers in Welding
Copyright © 2019 Andrea Vergun

ISBN: 9781688793781

Edited by Grace Warren
Cover Design by Madeleine Vergun

Available on Amazon.com

# Table of contents

# Preface

As an English as a Second Language (ESL) instructor, I wanted to add to the body of graded readers for English-language learners and new readers of English. Graded readers—books with grammar, vocabulary, and format modified to suit different reading abilities—are often scarce in ESL programs and community college libraries. In my own ESL classroom, I see how students truly enjoy choosing books at a comfortable reading level. Adult learners crave a variety of titles, genres, and levels to find books right for their reading ability and interests. This volume is suitable for ESL students at the upper-intermediate level and also appropriate for middle school-, high school-, or GED-level native-English speakers.

This book about welding careers and training aims to encourage students to consider welding as a college program. Often ESL students see English proficiency as their end goal, and have not considered going on to a college program. As ESL students approach the higher levels of English language ability, they should learn about what more is available to them and about the benefits of pursuing a college certificate or associate degree.

Welding is a worthwhile career to consider. Wages are good and the job outlook is strong. Many community colleges have welding programs, and students with a two-year associate degree are well trained in a variety of skills.

On another note, during my interviews with student and professional welders, I heard from many that they weren't cut out to go to a traditional four-year college. They liked working with their hands and building things. The traditional college route isn't for everyone, and the trades offer a solid alternative for a living-wage career.

By receiving career information in a graded reader, students can start envisioning themselves on a pathway to a career while they are still learning English. That pathway may mean more college studies for some, apprenticeships, or on-the-job training for others.

The book is presented in three parts. Part 1 provides career and training information. The format is designed to encourage reading for information, which might involve skimming for interesting topics and then reading in depth. Part 2 invites students to read the stories of actual students and professionals. The story titles and photos draw each reader to select the pieces that seem interesting to them. This section is formatted to encourage reading a story from beginning to end as a narrative. Part 3 is a section for interested students to learn more. There is a list of resources for further career exploration. A vocabulary section presents an opportunity to learn welding terms and new words that may be beyond the reader's current vocabulary range.

I began this project by presenting the idea to the welding department faculty at the community college where I teach ESL. They invited me to enroll in an introductory welding class so I could learn about welding by doing it myself. After participating in the welding class, I sat in on a fabrication course where I could continue learning and meet students who were in their second year of practice.

I interviewed more than a dozen students, instructors, and welding professionals and heard many stories of learning new skills and overcoming challenges. (I have changed their names for privacy.) Many have completed amazing projects or had unique opportunities; others are students poised to launch their careers. My most gratifying observation is that each welder seems to love what they are doing.

It is my hope that the reader will either see themselves in the background stories of these people, or envision themselves, in the future, as one of these successful professionals.

# Introduction

Have you ever noticed how many things are made of metal? Look around. Indoors, you can find chairs, desks, window frames, or lights. Outside, you can find cars, lamp posts, buildings, or bridges. Hidden behind walls or underground are pipes and metal beams. Metal is everywhere. Most metal **structures** and products are **welded** together.

## What is welding?

To **fabricate**, or make, most of these items, pieces of metal are cut, shaped, and then connected by welding. Welding is a process of joining metal together. Welders use very high heat to melt the metal at the joint, where the pieces fit together. Additional melted metal is added to the joint. As the melted metals cool, the two pieces stick together. The added metal becomes part of the two pieces making a strong connection.

There are many ways to weld. Welders use different tools, **equipment**, and processes for different metals and for different working conditions. On a windy **construction site**, a welder uses the welding process that is best for joining big **steel** beams together in those conditions. Meanwhile, in a shop, another welder uses a different process to weld thin sheet metal.

Welding is a career with many opportunities. There are a variety of industries, situations, and locations where welders can work. There is also opportunity to get higher-level positions with different responsibilities. Having a **trade**, or skill, such as welding, keeps you employed. A good welder can easily find work in another company or industry. Right now, there is a demand for welders in many different industries. It may be a good time to investigate a career in welding.

## What is in this book?

This book is for students who are thinking about next steps toward a career. First, the book provides information about welding careers and training at a **community college**. Second, welding **instructors**, students, and professionals tell about their welding experience and offer advice. Their stories may encourage you to think about welding. Finally, if you want to learn more, there is a chapter with ideas for exploring a welding career and training. Also, a vocabulary chapter provides the meanings for welding terms and new vocabulary. You can use it as a tool to learn new vocabulary.

### Common metals for welding

- **Steel** is a mix of iron and carbon. It is a strong metal that has a low cost. It is used in many structures and products such as buildings, machines, cars, etc.
- **Stainless steel** is a mix of steel and other metals. It is a strong metal that keeps its shine. It is used to make cookware, medical equipment, and tanks that store food or water.
- **Aluminum** is a light-weight metal used in the production of many products, for example, airplanes, outdoor furniture, and window frames.
- **Titanium** is light weight and very strong. It is used in making jet planes, rockets, military equipment, and medical implants such as artificial hips.

# Welds

A **weld** is the welded joint between two pieces of metal.

In some cases, a weld can be finished very smoothly. You cannot see that the pieces are welded together because the welder **grinds** down the weld. Grinding is the process of removing metal with power tools. It helps make parts look finished by taking away the extra metal left on top of the welded joint.

Many times, welds are not ground down. It is common to see the welds on structures such as bridges, where it is not important to grind the weld down.

A weld **bead** that is made carefully looks very neat.

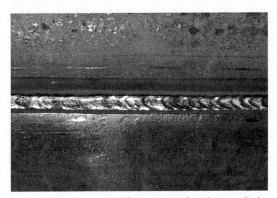

*A weld bead is melted filler metal that has cooled in the joint between the pieces of metal.*

# Part 1
# Welding careers and training

# Where do welders work and what do they do?

Welders have many opportunities for jobs. Welding is a skill that is used in a variety of industries for making products, building structures, or maintaining **facilities**. Welders can specialize their skills to work in different types of jobs.

Each industry, company, and project has its own way of working. It is not easy to describe what a welder does on a typical day because it is different for every industry.

## Industries that use welding

Welding is used in many industries. Manufacturing, or making products, is the number one use of welding, and manufacturing is done in different industries. Products can be any size from small electronic devices to huge ocean ships. Construction is the second biggest industry that employs welders. Construction includes making buildings, bridges, and highways. Many welders work in services such as maintaining or repairing buildings.

### Some industries that use welding

- construction: bridges, highways, buildings
- transportation: cars and trucks, trains, ships, airplanes
- manufacturing: products for consumers and other industries
- oil and gas: **pipelines**, facilities
- industrial shutdowns: repairing large facilities during a time that they close the building and stop all work

## Welder Fabricator

**Welder fabricator** is one type of welder's job. You may hear the term welder used for someone who is actually both welding and fabricating. A welder fabricator is a person who uses welding to fabricate, or make, things. These things may be structures or products.

To start, the welder fabricator looks at a plan for the project. The plan is called a **blueprint**. The blueprint contains information about how to make the item. It is a drawing with measurements and **symbols** that provide welding and building details. The welder fabricator uses the blueprint information to cut metal parts, and then bend, shape, fit, and weld them. During the **fabrication** process, the welder checks the welds to make sure they are done properly. They use power tools to finish the item, for example, using a grinder to remove extra metal to smooth the surface.

Grinding a weld

A fabricated part made from a blueprint

## Ironworker

**Ironworkers** are the people who build buildings, roads, and bridges. When you see a high-rise building being built in the city, you will see ironworkers. Sometimes you will see them working up high on steel beams.

There are many things ironworkers do on the job. In general, each workday they go to the construction location. They read instructions and blueprints for the project. They work with big pieces of heavy metal. The pieces of metal are usually too heavy to lift or carry by hand, so workers use equipment to lift and move them. The ironworkers weld the pieces together when they are in the correct position.

Ironworkers usually work outdoors as a team in all kinds of weather. However, they will not work if bad weather makes conditions too dangerous. They work in very high places, so working safely and using extra safety equipment is extremely important.

*An ironworker is wearing safety equipment for working on high buildings.*

## Working environments and locations

Welders can work outdoors or indoors. Some welders work outdoors on buildings, bridges, or pipelines. Weather and heights are concerns for the outdoor worker. Indoor workers may be in a busy, noisy industrial shop or, in contrast, in a clean, quiet high-tech manufacturing facility. Each workplace is different. Welders can even work underwater.

Welders can work near home or they can travel. Many cities have manufacturing companies that allow employees to work close to home. On the other hand, welders may travel to other places for work. For example, welders may go to natural gas pipeline locations, move to port cities for shipbuilding, or even travel to another country to work with the military.

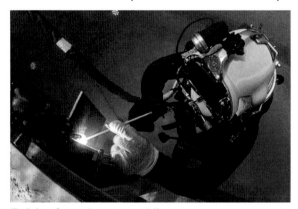

*Training for underwater welding*

*Working in a fabrication shop*

*An oil pipeline in Alaska*

*A two-level bridge for cars to cross the river*

*A water treatment plant with many pipes*

*Some projects need welders to work at night.*

*A welder joins sections of streetcar track together using equipment that heats the metal track and melts filler metal. The melted metal flows into the joint to weld the tracks together.*

# Reasons to consider welding

## Welders are in high demand

Right now, there is a shortage of welders. Many professional welders are retiring and there aren't enough young welders to replace them. So there is plenty of work to do. For example, the United States has very old buildings, bridges, highways, and other structures. We need welders to repair or replace them. Many other industries employ welders, too: construction, **automotive**, electric power, oil and natural gas, shipping, and manufacturing. In addition, welding is a growing profession, which means that companies will hire more welders.

## Job mobility

Having a trade, such as welding, gives you choices in work. A welder with good skills can change jobs within an industry or move to another industry. With welding skills, you can work as an employee, work for yourself, or be a company owner. Also, since welding is done all over the world, you can find jobs in other cities or in other countries.

## No college required

One good reason to become a welder is that a college degree is not required. Welders can get entry-level jobs with a high-school diploma or **GED (General Education Development)** and some training. Some companies will train workers on the job. People who get more training or complete school welding programs have more job options.

## Good pay

Experienced welders earn good pay. Of course, the pay depends on where you work and your skills. Some welding salaries are higher based on the type of job or the location. If you travel to places that have a high need for welders, you can earn very good money. For example, pipeline welding is a high-paying job, but it's necessary to travel to the location of the pipeline. Many jobs offer overtime work, which can add to the total pay.

## Advancement in the welding field

There are many different opportunities during a long welding career. Some people are happy to be welders for their whole career. Other people want to move into other welding positions. They may learn new welding skills on the job or in classes. They may take **certification** tests to show that they have the skills to qualify for different welding jobs. A welder who wants to have a management job can become a **supervisor** or manager. Welders can also study to become a **certified welding inspector**, a job with many different responsibilities, including checking parts for good quality welds. There are also good jobs working for the companies that make and sell welding equipment. A good sales person for a welding equipment company must know a lot about welding.

## A useful skill

Many people learn how to weld for reasons other than a career in welding. Some people weld for their hobbies, such as restoring old cars or making metal artwork. Other people use welding as an additional skill in their jobs. For example, a farmer may need to repair equipment on the farm.

## Welding off the job

Joe lives on a large property outside of the city. A few years ago, he bought a small plane that he flies from his home. Last year, he built a metal building to safely park his plane indoors. He used welding to **construct** the frame and make a large sliding door. Another project he welded was a metal rack for the back of his truck. He ties ropes to the rack to secure large loads. This keeps everything safely in the truck as he drives. He can even transport his plane with his truck. He puts the wings on the rack and the body on the trailer. He is not a professional welder, but he uses welding to fabricate and construct personal projects.

*Joe carries his plane on the truck's rack and trailer.*

# Is a career in welding a good choice for you?

Are you wondering if you might like to train to be a welder? Do you have some of these characteristics?

- You like to make things.
- You like working with your hands.
- You like to do work that is physical.
- You pay attention to details.
- You are a hard worker and always try to do your best.
- You can work by yourself or in a team.
- You communicate well with others.
- You like to solve problems.

They are some basic characteristics of good welders. Can you imagine yourself building things for a living? Read the descriptions about the physical, **accurate**, and creative work welders do.

## Welding is physical

Welders work with their hands to build things. Often they work with heavy materials and equipment, and may need physical strength to move them. Even if a welder works on small, light-weight parts, it is physical work using your hands in a skilled way.

On the job, welders may stand or sit for long periods of time, and need to keep their hands steady to produce good quality welds. Some welders work in small spaces or weld in awkward positions. In construction, a welder may work outside, high on a building, in bad weather.

Because welding is such physical work, it can become more difficult to do as you get older. Changes that happen with age, like stiff joints, unsteady hands, and poor **vision**, can make welding more difficult. One solution is to move up in your career as you age to supervisor or inspector. These jobs can be easier physically.

## Welding is accurate

Welders build things exactly to a plan. They must measure, cut, and weld carefully so that parts fit together perfectly. A small mistake in measuring can result in a big problem in the finished part. The welds must be good and strong without **defects** or weaknesses. The welder needs to pay attention to the quality of each weld. A bad weld needs to be removed and welded again.

## Welding is creative

Artists and people who like to weld things for themselves use their creativity with every project. On the job, welding can also be creative. Most projects require the welder to imagine the finished piece. Think about working from a blueprint. The drawing on the blueprint does not look like the finished product. Before starting, the welder needs to imagine the completed project in three dimensions (3-D). Also, welders need to think creatively about the best way to build the item.

*A detailed blueprint shows measurements, instructions, and different views of the part.*

# Training

## Focus on community college training programs

### What is a community college?

A community college is a two-year public educational institution that offers studies in many subjects. Some of the programs prepare students to transfer to a four-year college or university. Other programs prepare students to go directly into the workforce. The cost of attending a community college is much less than at a four-year college or university. In some places, similar schools are called junior colleges or trade colleges.

### Associate degree and certificate programs

Many community colleges offer a two-year **associate degree** in welding technology, as well as a **certificate of completion** for shorter programs. A certificate program prepares students for an entry-level welding job in a short amount of time. It is also a good way for working welders to learn new skills. Two-year associate degree students take a variety of welding and fabrication courses, as well as writing and math. They leave the college ready to work in different types of welding jobs.

### Classroom and shop

Students learn welding technology and related skills in the classroom and in the shop. In the classroom, instructors present new information, show real examples, introduce projects, and discuss safety. In the shop, students get hands-on experience by using the shop equipment to complete projects.

Students learn and practice many skills:

- welding
- blueprint reading
- fabrication
- **machining**
- quality **inspection**
- safety
- fitting
- computer skills
- technical math
- workplace writing

## Other courses are offered at a community college

Community colleges have many different areas of study, such as business, science, art, language, automotive, and health care. Because there are other classes at the school, students can learn more than one thing. For example, a student can take automotive repair or small business management classes while studying welding. Some community colleges combine departments, making it easy to learn more skills: welding/automotive or welding/machining, for example.

## Work experience

Students often work in a paid welding job while they are in school. They can get a job when they have enough skills to do the work. Some schools offer a course called **Cooperative Work Experience (CWE)**. In this course, a company hires a student to work, and the student earns college credit for the work. Some CWE jobs are paid, some are not. This is a great way to practice what you are learning and get real work experience.

## Additional resources at the college

Aside from welding classes, there are many resources and services for students at the community college:
- **financial aid** and **scholarships**
- career exploration
- personal **counseling**
- academic advising
- student clubs
- **English as a Second Language (ESL)** classes
- tutors
- library

# Planning for community college

## Time

Studying at a community college is a time commitment. To complete an associate degree in two years, you need to go to school full time. Full time means that you will have classes and lab for 12 or more hours a week, and you will have homework. Many students have a job, too. You need to coordinate your school and work schedules. If you have children, you may need to make plans for childcare or other help.

## Cost

Classes, books, and equipment can be expensive. Think about how you can pay for school. Most schools have financial aid that can help. Some trade organizations also give scholarships. Be sure to ask about possible sources of financial help at the school. Speak to the school's welding department instructors and someone at the financial aid office for information. Also ask about work-study jobs. These are part-time jobs at the college to help students earn money.

## Motivation

Going to school takes a lot of time and money. To be successful, you need to be **motivated**, or have a strong interest, to come to class and complete the projects. Some students get discouraged or frustrated when they have difficulties. They feel like quitting. Remember that you are learning a new skill. It takes time and practice. Keep up with the class projects and the homework. Get help from instructors and tutors if you need it.

If you have some problems at home or with school, you may lose motivation. The college has resources to help, for example, counseling and advising services. You can talk to someone who can help you to find solutions.

# Other training options

## Private trade school

Trade schools focus on preparing their students for a career. Students have classroom time and lots of hands-on practical courses. A trade school program can take less time than a community college program, so students may be in a job sooner. Trade schools can be expensive, but they usually offer scholarships and financial aid.

## On-the-job training

Sometimes a company hires people who have little or no welding experience. The company teaches the employee the skills needed for the job. One advantage is that the employee can make money while they learn.

## Apprenticeship

An **apprenticeship** is a training program where the **apprentice**, or learner, learns while working. It is usually a program offered by a trade organization. Beginners learn from professionals and may also take classes. Apprenticeships usually last a few years. Apprentices earn money while they learn, and at the same time they get real job experience. They earn more money as they get more experience. When they complete their training, they will become a **journeyman** and receive full pay. A person must apply for an apprenticeship. It is often helpful to have some skills before applying.

Zack, Welding Student

I already had a lot of experience welding when I graduated high school. I could have started working as a welder. However, I decided to go to the community college to get my associate degree. With a degree, I will have more job options and job promotion opportunities. Before completing my degree, I will also get American Welding Society certification in stainless steel welding and structural welding to show employers that I have these skills.

David, Professional Welder

I trained on the job. It was great because I didn't have any welding training before I started, just some experience. I have learned a lot at the company. Now I can weld, fabricate, cut, **lay out**, order, and supervise.

Pete, Professional Welder

I went to an automotive trade school where students usually learn how to manufacture cars for big car companies. My plan was to learn how to build race cars. I was motivated and completed the training in one year. It is very hard to get a job with a race team because there just aren't many jobs. My instructor thought my skills were good, so he recommended me for a job. After showing my skills, I was hired as a welder by a race team, just one week after graduation!

Going to a trade school was exactly what I needed to get my dream job. But I only learned how to weld for one type of job. I knew how to weld well, but I wanted to know more. After I left that job, I took some welding and fabrication classes at a community college to learn more so I could work in different industries.

# Essential skills on the job

## Communication in English

Clear communication is very important on the job. If you speak your native language better than English, you can still find work as a welder. However, it is important to have a comfortable level of English. Workers must be able to understand instructions and communicate with all co-workers and supervisors. If English is not your first language, ESL classes can help you build skill and confidence.

Even if you speak English as your first language, it is important to communicate clearly. One very important reason is safety. If someone needs help or needs to warn a co-worker, they must say it clearly, and the co-worker must understand.

If you speak two languages, you may find welding jobs where you can use both languages. Being bilingual is an advantage.

## Reading and writing

Welders only need to do a little reading and writing on the job. They read written instructions or blueprints for the job. Blueprints are mainly symbols, drawings, and measurements. Blueprint reading is taught and practiced in welding training programs. A supervisor needs to read and write more. They read detailed instructions and messages from management, and they write short reports and material orders. Jobs in management or inspecting require much more reading and writing.

## Math

Welders use math every day. Measuring with a **tape measure** or other tools is an important skill. Everything must be measured accurately. Often, measurements need to be added together to know the final length of a part. This includes adding fractions.

Geometry is another math skill to learn. Welders work with angles, circles, area, and volume. A technical math class or shop math class teaches the math that welders use.

Craig, Welding Instructor

Carefully check your measurements. Make sure everything is exactly the right size. Start doing this when you are training because on the job, you need to have high-quality work.

Also, you must communicate clearly with your co-workers. Misunderstandings can create dangerous situations.

Daniel, Certified Welding Inspector

I am an inspector at a company that makes military equipment. Part of my job is to check everyone's welding to make sure that it is done properly. There are many essential skills that I use on the job. I read blueprints to know how the part should be built. I use math when I take accurate measurements of the parts using different kinds of tools. I write a detailed report after I **inspect** the work. My reports must be written very neatly with correct spelling. I need to communicate clearly with many different people. I'm bilingual, and knowing Spanish is useful on the job.

David, Professional Welder

In my job, I use math and measurements to figure out how many parts I can cut from a piece of sheet metal. I want to get as many pieces on each sheet as possible so I don't waste metal. I also need to calculate how many sheets to order for the products we are making.

Spanish is my strongest language. I use it to speak with my co-workers, but I need to speak English with my boss. It took a while, but now I speak English well.

I didn't do any writing when I was just welding, but when I started doing cutting, I needed to write. That's when I started taking ESL classes. I needed to improve my vocabulary.

# Safety first, safety always

There are many possible dangers in the welding profession. Some common safety concerns are extreme heat, very bright light, and loud noise. Also, welding can add dangerous chemical gases to the air. Welders must follow the safety rules to stay safe in any situation.

## Personal Protective Equipment

Welders need to protect their bodies while in work areas. Every welder should use **Personal Protective Equipment (PPE)**. Examples of PPE are **welding helmets**, safety glasses, gloves, proper clothing, safety boots, and hearing protection.

### Welding helmets and clothing

Welding equipment makes an extremely bright light called an **arc**. Like the sun, it can damage the eyes or create a sunburn on the skin. While welding, welders must protect their skin with proper clothing, and their face, neck, and eyes with a welding helmet. The helmet covers the face and neck and has a very dark window that blocks much of the light. Other types of welding glasses can also be used to protect against the harmful light.

Welding melts metal at very high temperatures. The hot metal can burn the skin, and **sparks**, or small bits of hot metal, can fall on clothing. To prevent burns or fires, welders must wear proper clothing. Leather gloves protect the hands from the heat. For

*This welder is wearing PPE: safety glasses, welding helmet, jacket, jeans, work boots, and gloves.*

more protection, welders wear cotton jeans, long-sleeve cotton shirts, and a leather or cotton jacket. Strong work boots protect the feet from sparks and heavy objects.

### Safety glasses

One of the most important pieces of PPE is a pair of safety glasses. Safety glasses are strong plastic glasses that protect the eyes from sparks, metal dust, or sharp objects in the welding shop. Workers should always wear them in the work area.

### Hearing protection

The shop is a very loud place when workers are using power tools, hammers, and equipment. Metal is noisy, too. Big pieces of metal make noise when they are put down or hit other metal pieces. The noise can damage your hearing over time. It is important to wear ear plugs if you are around loud noises for long periods of time.

## A safe workplace

The high heat from welding can create chemical gases that are harmful to breathe. Also, metal dust from cutting or grinding can float in the air. Welding shops must have good **ventilation** to move the harmful air out of the area.

The shop must have other safety equipment such as first aid kits and fire extinguishers. Every company should have a safety program and train employees about how to stay safe. There is a government agency that works with companies to help them have a safe environment.

## Safety while training and on the job

Mike, Welding Instructor

Welders work with heavy steel, and it's easy to get injured. I tell students to watch what other people are doing to make sure their co-workers are working safely. If other people are not being safe, their actions may hurt you. Also, keep your workspace neat. You don't want to trip on metal or electric cords.

James, Certified Welding Inspector

There are many safety rules around welding job sites. You must follow the rules, even if no one else is. You need to take care of yourself. Wear your PPE. Always wear your safety glasses because the most common injury is to the eye. Also, remember that the metal is sharp and it is easy to cut your hands if you are not wearing gloves.

When you go to a new place to work, ask the company about their safety program. If they don't have one, it is not a good place to work. They should care about your safety.

Julie, Professional Welder

At the company I worked for, we had equipment to move heavy materials to our work stations. I always used it because I didn't want to get injured from lifting heavy things by myself.

Pete, Professional Welder

My company is very strict about safety. We are not allowed to lift anything over 35 pounds by ourselves. There are different types of equipment for that. Also, we must report every injury. I burned my finger one time. It didn't seem serious, but I had to fill out a report about it. One thing that I liked, however, was that they asked me to suggest changes to prevent this kind of injury in the future.

# Advice from students, instructors, and professionals

## Don't give up!

You won't be great at welding in the beginning. It is a skill that you need to practice, just like playing a guitar or drawing. The more time you weld, the better you will be. You will get better every time you sit down and weld.

## Look for financial aid

Most students can get financial aid, which is money to help pay for school. Many schools and trade organizations offer scholarships, money that you don't need to pay back. You usually need to apply for the scholarships, but it is worth it. Ask your school about scholarships and other financial aid.

It is a good idea to work in a welding company while you are in school. You can earn money and get experience while you finish your studies.

## Get help for difficult classes

If you have difficulty understanding the reading, doing the math, or writing in the classes, you can get help. One idea is to make a study group with classmates to help each other.

If you are taking a math class and you don't understand, get help. Ask the instructor or see if your school has free math tutors.

If English is not your first language, you could take an ESL class to improve your skills. Also, you can talk in English with your classmates to practice the vocabulary and language of welding.

## Network!

Try to network, that is, meet and talk to a lot of people in your classes and in the welding profession. When you are at school, put your phone away! Use your free time to talk to classmates. Share information about welding, companies, and jobs. Many people get jobs by talking to people they meet in class. If you are working, make friends with your co-workers. You may want to call them in the future when you need a job.

## Learn about jobs

Go to job fairs at your school or in the community. A job fair is an event for people to learn about different companies and career opportunities. At the job fair, each company has a table with information and a person to talk to. Ask questions and see if the company is a good place for you to work.

## Plan for the next job

Once you are in a job, think about what you want to do next. What would you like to do one year from now or in five years? Then, take actions toward that goal.

Take advantage of every opportunity while you are in a job. Learn as much as you can. This will help you to move into new positions or earn more money.

# Women in welding

## A shortage of welders

There are great opportunities for women to go into welding. The population of welders is getting older and many are retiring. Fewer young people are choosing to go into the trades, so there is a shortage of welders. There are not enough workers to do the work. Many companies want to hire more welders, and they welcome both well-trained men and women.

## Consider the trades

Welding, as most of the trades, has been mainly a man's profession, but that may be slowly changing. More women are going into the trades than before. They have good reasons to consider the trades. First, the jobs are available and the pay is good. Also, many women like working with their hands, just as men do. It's a satisfying and creative job. Welders say that they get satisfaction when they complete projects and can see the results of their hard work. They use creative thinking to find the best way to build something and to solve problems as they work.

## Some concerns

It is true that welding has been a man's world, and the workplace culture can be difficult for women. The reality is that some women report **harassment** by men on the job. Some women have experienced **discrimination**, meaning that they are treated differently than their male co-workers. For example, some women are not given the same training as men, or they are not given good work assignments because they are women.

## A new culture

Hopefully, as more and more women enter welding and other trades, it will become more normal, and women will be treated as professionals and equals in every workplace. Additionally, as a new generation of welders replaces those who are retiring, the culture can change.

## Advice to women interested in a woman-friendly workplace

- Network with other women welding students or professionals to learn about workplaces that they like, or don't like.

- Go to job fairs and talk to the people from different companies. They can tell you about their workplace. Ask about the number of women who work in welding at the company.

- Talk with your instructors about companies in the area. They have relationships with local employers.

- Contact an organization for women in the trades for information.

# Conclusion to Part 1

Now that you have read a little bit about welding as a career and ways to train for it, read the stories in Part 2. They are short stories based on the actual experiences of welding students and professionals. The students tell how they decided to train in welding. The professionals' stories show a variety of jobs and experiences. Look at the titles and photos to see which stories interest you.

*A new bridge for people, bikes, buses, and streetcars*

*Welds on the new bridge*

# Part 2
# Student and professional stories

# Taking advantage of every opportunity

Julian was taking ESL classes when he received an email with a great opportunity. The email invited him to start a special program to work toward a welding degree at the community college. It looked interesting, but he didn't think his English was good enough to take college classes. He had been in the United States for only four years, and had only studied English for two years. Also, he didn't have much free time. He went to English classes in the evening, after working all day.

Julian asked for more information about the opportunity. He found out that it was a program for ESL and GED students to study welding full time and also get help with reading, writing, and math. He thought it would be a good opportunity to start a strong career, so he decided to quit his job and learn how to weld.

When he started the welding classes, he was uncomfortable. He was the only Spanish speaker in the class, so he had to use English. Also, the **textbook** was difficult to read, and he had so much homework.

Soon he became friends with other students. He learned a lot more English just by talking with his classmates. They made a study group to help each other with the reading and the homework.

While he was taking classes, he had a part-time job, so he had to manage his time carefully. He decided to make Sundays his homework days. Every Sunday, he completed all the homework for the next week.

When Julian finishes the program in a few months, he wants to work where he can use all of the skills and knowledge he has learned. He wants to find a job where he can continue to learn and improve his skills.

His advice is to go to school to learn something new, even if you don't speak English well. Imagine how a degree can lead to a better life. Apply for scholarships with the school, the department, or a local trade organization to help with the costs. Take advantage of every opportunity.

# Practice makes perfect

Alex lost his job as a machine operator a few years ago, but his bad luck gave him a new career. He spoke to someone at the employment office in his state because he needed a new job. They told him that he qualified for help to train for a new trade. They told him about a special welding program at the community college. In this program, the students would learn welding while working towards earning a GED. He was excited to learn something new, and he needed a GED.

One thing Alex likes about the welding program is that the classes are "hands on." Students learn skills by working in the shop, and the teachers are there to help. He enjoys building things. At first, he was frustrated because his welds were not very good, but he was patient with himself. He practiced and practiced until he could make good welds. Now he is very happy with his skills and he is able to quickly complete the class welding projects. With his extra time, he learns new skills and makes his own projects in the shop.

For Alex, welding is now easy, but fabrication can still be challenging. To build something from a blueprint, he has to imagine the final piece before he starts working. He needs to read the blueprint information very carefully and measure everything accurately. All of the parts of the project need to fit perfectly. He gets better and better at fabrication with each class he takes.

Alex has done very well in the welding program. He has gotten A grades in all of his classes, including math and writing. He also completed his GED while studying for the welding degree. He is very motivated because he has a goal for a better future. He feels good being back in school; something he never thought would happen.

# Training projects

Students practice welding and fabricating skills in the shop by building objects from a blueprint or other instructions. As students get experience, they can design their own projects.

An example project for a fabrication class is the cube. To make the cube, students start with six-inch square pieces of steel sheet metal. They must think about a way to hold the metal pieces carefully in place as they weld the outside joints. When all edges are welded, students grind down the welds so they are not visible. The final cube has a smooth surface and edges.

*A student project in progress (left photo) and completed (right photo)*

# Leaving a small town for a better future

Ashley didn't know what she wanted to do after high school. The only job she could find in her small town was working at a pizza restaurant. She didn't want to work in a low-paying job for the rest of her life. After a few years, she decided to go to a community college to get a degree in welding. She chose welding because she already knew how to weld a little. She had welded in her high school metal shop. She also knew that welding is a job that pays well.

To go to the college, she had to leave her small town. She sold everything and moved near the college. She wasn't working, so she applied for financial aid to pay for classes and supplies.

Ashley decided to complete the full two-year degree program so she would have strong skills and good job opportunities. She also wants to be able to move up in a company to get a better job and to make more money. Having a degree will give her an advantage.

Now Ashley is working at a welding company and going to school at the same time. Her workplace has a mix of men and women, and she feels like she is part of a team.

Ashley is glad that she didn't go to college right after she graduated from high school. Starting college a few years later was a good decision for her. She didn't know what she wanted to study after high school, and she is happy that she waited until she had a plan.

# A good start made better with a degree

Zack learned how to weld on projects at home when he was nine years old. In high school, he took metal shop classes, where he learned more about welding. In class, students had to develop their own projects. He decided to make an art sculpture, and people really liked it. His art teacher asked him to make a metal sculpture for her, and so did his grandfather. During high school, he worked in his grandfather's shop doing high-quality welding on stainless steel. Now, while he's in college, he works at a metal fabrication company.

Zack has always been a hard worker and takes pride in his work. In high school, he completed several college-level classes so he wouldn't have to take them and pay for them in college. However, during his last year in high school, he was not sure he wanted to go to college. He was already doing professional welding. He thought maybe he could just start working in a shop instead.

Zack's father advised him to go to college. His father explained that a degree would be very valuable in getting a good job and having more opportunities in the future. Zack agreed with that advice. He decided to go to the community college to earn an associate degree in welding.

He is almost finished with the program. Before he graduates, he plans to take the tests for certification in different kinds of welding. Certification shows you have a certain skill, and some employers require it. Zack wants to be certified in structural steel welding because the construction business is strong. He also wants to be certified in the stainless-steel welding that he learned at his grandfather's business.

At 19 years old, Zack is already welding at a professional level. With his work experience, his certifications, and his degree, Zack is in a good position to have a successful career in the welding and fabricating industry.

# A new country and a new skill

David came to the United States 13 years ago. He worked in accounting in his home country but could not get an accounting job in the United States. He had to think of a different job that paid well. He knew a little about welding because he used welding to make and fix things at home. So when he came to the United States, he was able to get an entry-level welding job. When he started, his boss trained him. During the years he has worked at the company, he has learned how to fabricate all of their products. He quickly became very good at his job and took on more and more responsibility.

David has many job skills beyond welding and fabricating that are useful in his work. For one, he is able to use his Spanish on the job to communicate easily with the other Spanish speakers. He supervises other welders and helps them if they have trouble with their work.

He is also very good at math. One way he uses math is to plan the best way to cut many different parts from one big sheet of metal. As part of his work fabricating products, he carefully measures and lays out the part patterns on the sheet metal so he doesn't waste supplies. He also uses math to order the correct amount of materials for making the products.

Nowadays David trains new workers for his employer, yet he still takes every opportunity to learn new things himself. He wants to learn additional welding and fabrication skills. In the future, he may take a class or join another company to do different kinds of projects. He already has many important skills that would be welcome at another company, but learning new skills is always a great idea.

# Taking her skills to a new generation

Julie is a woman in the trades. She is a skilled welder fabricator now teaching others how to weld. However, it wasn't easy for her to get where she is today.

When she was around 18 years old, she decided that she wanted to be an auto mechanic, fixing cars. She took an automotive class, but the teacher wasn't ready for a woman to work as an auto mechanic. He gave her a bad grade, even though her work was good. Julie was so frustrated that she left school.

After that, she worked many different jobs, some in the automotive industry, and others not. She never worked as an auto mechanic. That dream faded.

Many years later, she went back to the community college to complete her studies. She took a welding class because she wanted to learn how to take old furniture and make something new and different. She was very good at welding, even as a beginner. She decided to get her degree in welding and work as a welder fabricator.

She faced a few problems as a woman in welding shops, but they didn't stop her. In one shop, she was told by other workers that she wasn't strong enough to do the work. However, she easily moved heavy metal pieces using the equipment in the shop. In another job, the employees were told they must work 11-hour days. Julie had small children at home, and so it was very difficult for her to be there from morning until night.

Julie left that job when she was invited to be a teaching assistant in the community college welding department. It opened a new opportunity for her. Now she's teaching welding classes at the college. While she's working at the college, she's also completing her training to be a Career and Technical Education instructor for high school welding programs.

In her job as an instructor, she can encourage young women interested in a welding career. Her advice is to pursue a welding career if you want one, and don't let anyone tell you can't do something because you're a woman. Have confidence in yourself and your work.

# A dream come true

Pete, his wife, and young children packed up the car and drove 3,000 miles east to build a new life. He originally had a job in construction in California, but he had to quit because he badly injured his knee and back. He was out of work for a very long time. After recovering, he got a job as a supervisor at a golf course, but he couldn't make enough money to support his family. He had to find another way.

Pete always loved car racing. He decided that for his next career, he wanted to build race cars—NASCAR race cars. NASCAR is the National Association for Stock Car Auto Racing. The center of the NASCAR racing industry is in North Carolina, a state on the east coast of the United States.

He applied to an automotive trade school in North Carolina that trains people to work in the automotive manufacturing industry. The school also has a special program to train students to build NASCAR cars.

When Pete and his family arrived in North Carolina, he started taking classes. He was excited to go back to school. He was so motivated about his new opportunity that he earned an A grade in every class.

When he finished school, his skills were excellent. A NASCAR racing team quickly hired him to build cars. He used the skills he learned in his classes to weld and fabricate the cars.

Each racing team has many cars. His team had 18. Drivers race each car about six times and then stop using it. Pete was always busy making or repairing cars for the team. All of the cars looked similar on the outside, but he built them differently for each type of race. For example, he built some cars for short races with tight turns, and others for high-speed races on long, straight tracks. The fabrication team always thought about ways to make each car better and faster.

*A NASCAR race*

These race cars were expensive. A NASCAR car cost over $200,000 to design and build. The shop where he built these amazing machines was always neat and clean. It looked like a luxury-car showroom.

Pete loved working for a winning race team, especially the excitement of watching his powerful cars reach speeds close to 200 miles per hour on the race track. He knows that he made the right decision to move his family across the country to pursue his dream job.

# Titanium welding—a new challenge

It's been several years since Pete left his dream job with a NASCAR race team. However, Pete has a new job now and he's pretty excited about it. He's welding titanium, a very strong, light-weight metal. It's used in the **aerospace**, **aviation**, and military industries because of its strength and light weight. He's working on large airplane engine parts.

He found the job by talking to a friend in class. Pete found out that this friend worked at a very good company. He asked him how to get a job there, and his friend showed him the website and open jobs. Pete applied online and the company soon asked him to come to talk with them. He met with a manager and then took a welding test to show them his skills. He did well on the test, and the company hired him. Welding titanium is a special skill and requires a welder to work in an unusual way, so Pete will get additional training as he works.

This job is difficult because of the unusual set-up. The part that Pete welds must be protected from the air because air can damage the titanium during welding. Welders usually place the part inside a closed box, called a **chamber**, and a special gas replaces the air. At this company, the chamber is big enough to hold an airplane engine part.

Because Pete cannot be in the chamber himself, he must weld from outside. To weld, he sticks his hands into gloves that go through the wall of the chamber. Welding this way is hard because he cannot easily see what he is working on. The wall of the chamber prevents him from looking at the part from above or behind. He uses mirrors inside the chamber to see around the part when he welds. He watches what he is welding in the mirror. As a result, he is welding backwards; everything is in reverse. He says he will need lots of practice for his eyes and hands to get used to welding this way.

In this particular job, Pete is not joining two pieces of metal together in the usual way. He is adding metal to areas of the part that are not perfectly level with the surface. To understand this, imagine a different kind of example, a pothole in the street. The street has a spot that is not level with the rest of the road. The road maintenance people come to fill it and smooth it so the road is level. Pete is using welding to melt and add metal to the low spots in the part. Later, another worker will use tools to grind down the extra metal so the surface is smooth and even.

Pete likes this job. He is excited to apply his skills to something new and challenging. He is happy that he asked his classmate about jobs at the company.

*This welder is filling the holes in a small titanium part, as Pete does. The welder is not using a welding chamber for this job. A special gas comes out of the hand-held equipment to protect the melted metal from the air.*

# Making art for the world to see

Imagine large metal sculptures that move with the wind or have mechanical parts. What would it take to make this kind of sculpture? Often, the artist has the idea, and the welder fabricator has the skill to make the idea real.

When Craig first started welding, he began to think about welding for art. He decided it was something he wanted to do. He set his mind on that goal and things started to fall into place. He met a sculpture artist and volunteered to work without pay. Craig made large metal art pieces for indoor art shows and outdoor public spaces like parks or plazas. Soon he was getting paid for his excellent work.

To start a new project, an artist gives Craig a drawing or small model of the sculpture. It usually doesn't have much detail. It is up to Craig to think about the best way to build it. Since each sculpture is unique, Craig must think of unique solutions.

If the artist wants it to have moving parts, Craig needs to think about how to make them work. For example, if the sculpture is a flying bird, he must think of a way to move the wings up and down. He has to think like an engineer to plan for both the art and the movement. He often makes his own mechanical parts because he can't just go to the hardware store to buy them. He enjoys working on these challenging projects and learning new things as he works.

He usually welds and fabricates the sculptures with a partner or a small team in a big indoor space. If the sculpture is big, he makes it in smaller pieces indoors, and then brings the pieces outdoors to the sculpture's permanent place. Once there, he uses equipment to lift the heavy pieces and hold them in place so he can weld them together.

He always needs to consider his own safety while he's working, as well as the safety of the public when the sculpture is finished. Additionally he needs to make sure the sculpture will be safe. It may be outside in strong wind or floating on the water. Craig needs to think about these concerns as he works.

Fabricating sculptures has been an exciting part of Craig's career. He likes the opportunity to be creative and to solve interesting problems. He has been able to travel across the country and overseas to build art pieces and then to repair them if they get damaged. Craig works hard to make the sculptures perfect so the public can enjoy them. He takes pride in his work and looks forward to every challenge.

*A large steel art sculpture represents a building that used to be in that place. It is in Portland, Oregon.*

# From welder to business owner

Sometimes bad situations can motivate you to do great things! Jason built his own successful business after losing his job. He lost his job, but he kept his welding and fabrication skills. His skills and hard work turned into his own company.

Jason didn't expect to have a welding career. After graduating from high school, he went to a university because his parents expected him to go. He got good grades in university classes, but he wasn't interested in studying there. He wanted to make and build things with his hands. During his third year, he quit school and got a job.

His interest in welding began when he wanted to make a metal part for his car, but he didn't know how to use welding equipment. He took a welding class at a community college to learn some basic skills. He quickly discovered that he was very good at welding and he loved it. He completed the welding program in only a year and a half. When he graduated, he got a job at a company that fabricates big metal tanks for making beer and wine.

After working there for five years, Jason was laid off because the company didn't have enough work for everyone. However, people that he knew started asking him if he could make beer tanks for them. He had the knowledge and skill to fabricate the tanks, and he could build the large tanks in his garage.

His friends were very happy with the tanks and told other beer makers about Jason's work. More and more people asked him to build tanks for them, and pretty soon, he was using both his own and his friend's garage to keep up with demand. His business grew so much that he had to hire workers and rent a real shop. He opened his business with about ten welders. He had so many orders that customers had to wait up to six months for their tanks to be finished. Now his company is also making tanks for the first company he worked for. They have too many orders and need his help. Business is good!

*A beer brewery is setting up new tanks from Jason's shop. It took about 250 hours to make these four stainless steel tanks.*

Owning and running a business was new to Jason. Sometimes it was very stressful. He had no business experience, but he has created a very successful company. As a business owner, his job now is not welding but keeping his welders busy with work. He loves being able to employ others who enjoy welding as much as he does.

His advice to students is to remain friends with your past co-workers and employers. You never know if you will need their help or work for them again in the future. He also encourages students to learn a trade, such as welding. It is something that you will always have. If you lose your job, you can still practice your trade. You can even open your own business.

*Mike's Barracuda is a work in progress.*

# Restoring classic cars

Each time that Mike works on restoring his classic Barracuda car, he feels pride in his work. It's a challenging project, but he knows that he will do high-quality work. Barracudas were made in the 1960s and 1970s. These cars were beautiful, powerful, and fast. They got everyone's attention when they drove down the street. The car company stopped making Barracudas in 1974. People who collect old cars still love the Barracuda. They want to restore the cars to look like new.

Mike's car is close to 50 years old and needs repairs to the engine, the frame, and the body. He looks for original parts to replace the ones damaged or missing. To repair the body and other metal parts, he needs to use his welding skills.

To start, he cuts and removes damaged pieces of metal. Then he cuts new pieces from a sheet of the same thickness. The pieces need to fit perfectly, so he measures and shapes them until they match the hole he has made. He then carefully welds the new pieces in place. Finally, he grinds down the extra metal so the surface is smooth. Each weld must be finished so that it is impossible to see that a new piece has been added. He's been working on this car for a long time. When he finishes, the car will be beautiful again.

For now, the Barracuda "lives" in the community college's automotive department. Mike is a welding instructor at the same community college, and often brings his students to see the work he is doing on the car. With his car, he shows the students that welding is a skill for someone who wants to restore cars as a job or as a hobby.

# Becoming a welding inspector

Daniel completed his military service and returned to the United States from Iraq, and he asked himself, "Now what do I do?" He and his wife were expecting a baby and he needed to make some decisions—and some money. He didn't have a college degree. He had joined the military immediately after graduating from high school, and had been sent to Iraq. What job could he do that would support his family?

Home again, Daniel remembered that he had liked making metal art in high school. He did some research and decided to go to school for a degree in welding. He knew it could help him get a job that paid well.

In the past, he had hated school, but now he was motivated to succeed because he had a family to support. He did very well in the welding program. With every project, he focused on details and learned as much as he could.

One day, a welding inspection company came to the college. They were looking for people to train as inspectors. Usually, inspectors are welders who have many years of experience in the trade. Inspectors look for problems in welded materials, so they need to know a lot about welding and metals. However, the company could not find enough inspectors to serve their many clients. The company decided to train new welders who had learned a variety of welding skills in school.

Daniel applied for the job. After months of training and then testing, he got the job as a Certified Welding Inspector. First, he did visual inspecting, looking at welds for problems. Later he learned how to find problems in the welds using electronic equipment. If he finds a weld with problems, the workers must remove the weld and do it again. The job is very important because a bad weld could be dangerous. Imagine the danger of a bridge falling down because the metal is not joined securely. The welds must be perfect.

In his first job as an inspector, Daniel traveled all over the country to inspect military equipment and facilities. Now he is an inspector at a company that makes military equipment. He doesn't have to travel for his job, so he can be at home every night with his family.

# Part 3
# Learn more

# Exploring further

If you are interested in a welding career, don't stop after reading this book. Keep learning! Talk to people. Look at the information on websites. Starting anything new can be hard, but here are ideas to help you find more information about welding training and work.

## School resources

Contact these people or departments at a community college or other school near you for information about careers and study programs:

- A career coach, academic advisor, or guidance counselor can help you explore a variety of possible careers and areas of study.
- The welding department can provide information about the program, classes, and career opportunities in the area.
- The ESL department can guide you if you would like to strengthen your English-language skills.
- The GED program or department can give you information if you did not finish high school.

## Career information

Read information on these websites to learn more about welding as a career:

- **CareerOneStop, www.careeronestop.org**
  Enter the word *welding* in the search box. Read information about different careers, including descriptions, pay, training options, and links to other resources.
- **Bureau of Labor Statistics, www.bls.gov**
  Enter the word *welding* in the search box. Then read information on the Occupational Outlook Handbook pages.

## Welding organization

American Welding Society (AWS), www.aws.org
AWS is an important organization for the welding profession.

Topics on the website include
- careers
- education, including on-line courses
- certification
- books and other publications
- standards, that is rules and practices in the welding trade
- student membership in the organization
- scholarships
- events

## Women in the trades

There are several organizations for women in the trades. They have information about apprenticeship programs, pre-apprenticeship training programs, the trades in general, workplace rights, and more.

Some example organizations:
- Oregon Tradeswomen, Inc., http://www.tradeswomen.net/
- Tradeswomen, Inc., http://tradeswomen.org/
- Chicago Women in Trades, https://cwit.org/

## Apprenticeships

To learn more about apprenticeships in general, see the U.S. Department of Labor's website at https://www.apprenticeship.gov/become-apprentice.

# Vocabulary

## Acronyms

**CWE:** Cooperative Work Experience.
**ESL:** English as a Second Language.
**GED:** General Education Development.
**PPE:** Personal Protective Equipment.

## Vocabulary

**accurate:** (adjective) without mistakes, correct.

**aerospace:** (noun) the industry related to making airplanes, jets, rockets, missiles, etc.

**aluminum:** (noun) a light-weight metal used to make many products, for example, bicycles, outdoor furniture, and window frames.

**apprentice:** (noun) a person who learns from a more experienced person; a person participating in an apprenticeship.

**apprenticeship:** (noun) a position where a beginner, an apprentice, learns a trade from a more experienced person.

**arc:** (noun) the very bright light produced while welding with electricity; the arc is electricity that creates heat to melt the metal; it can cause eye damage and sunburn to the skin.

**associate degree:** (noun) a two-year degree offered at community colleges as well as some other types of schools and colleges.

**automotive:** (noun) the industry related to motor vehicles, including cars, trucks, buses, etc.

**aviation:** (noun) the industry related to aircraft, including airplanes, jets, helicopters, military aircraft, etc.

**bead:** (noun) the cooled filler metal in a weld joint; beads usually have a neat pattern as the welder carefully moves the heat source and adds melted filler metal along the joint.

**blueprint:** (noun) a plan for building a product, part, or structure; a blueprint for welding includes a flat drawing of the part with information about how to build it; the blueprint can show the structure from different points of view, provide measurements, and show the type of welds and bends needed to make the part, among other things.

**certificate of completion:** (noun) a document given to students who finish a program of study to show that they finished; a certificate program can be up to two years of study, but is usually shorter than an associate degree.

**certification:** (noun) the process of getting a certificate, which is a document showing that a person has a skill; in the case of welding certification, a welder takes a test to show that he or she can perform certain welding skills at a professional level. When they pass the test, they receive a certificate.

**certified:** (adjective) having a certificate; someone is certified in a welding skill when they have passed the certification tests related to that skill.

**certified welding inspector:** (noun) a professional who has the responsibility to check and measure welding quality, watch workplace safety, review documents, test welders for certification, and much more.

**chamber:** (noun) a room or large box with a special use; in titanium welding, an enclosed box without oxygen where the titanium is welded.

**community college:** (noun) a two-year public school that offers studies in many subjects; students can earn associate degrees and certificates of completion; similar schools are called junior college or trade college.

**construct:** (verb) to build.

**construction:** (noun) industry related to building structures, including houses, office buildings, bridges, etc.

**Cooperative Work Experience:** (noun) a community college class in which students earn college credit while working at a company.

**counseling:** (noun) guidance and advice from professionals to help people solve problems; a community college often has counseling services for students.

**defect:** (noun) a feature or quality that makes something imperfect; a defect in a weld can be a serious problem; it can make the joint weak and unstable.

**discrimination:** (noun) the act of treating someone differently and unfairly because of race, sex, age, etc.; in some cases, discrimination can be illegal.

**equipment:** (noun) devices used to perform a task; for welding, equipment could be the protective personal equipment such as safety glasses and a helmet, the welding machine, other machines or tools used in the welding shop, lifting devices such as cranes or forklifts, etc.

**English as a Second Language:** (noun) English as taught to people who speak a different language; community colleges often offer ESL classes for different language abilities.

**fabricate:** (verb) to make, build, or construct from different pieces.

**fabrication:** (noun) the act of making, building, or constructing something from different pieces.

**facility:** (noun) a place that is for a specific purpose, for example, a manufacturing facility, a water treatment facility, a research facility, etc.

**financial aid:** (noun) money for students in college, trade schools, universities, etc. to help pay for the cost of going to school; it can be provided as loans that the student pays back, grants and scholarships that the student does not pay back, or work-study jobs.

**General Educational Development:** (noun) a group of tests that shows a person has high school level academic skills; for people who did not complete high school; students can take classes to study for the tests at a community college or other place; when the student passes all of the tests, they receive a GED certificate.

**grind:** (verb) in welding, to remove metal from a surface using a special power tool called a grinder.

**harassment:** (noun) rude actions or words directed at someone that are based on race, sex, age, etc.; in some cases, harassment can be illegal.

**inspect:** (verb) to examine something carefully; in welding, it is to check to see if a part is welded and built correctly.

**inspection:** (noun) the act of inspecting; an inspection can be visual (by looking), with electronic instruments, or other ways.

**instructor:** (noun) a teacher; community college teachers are usually called instructors.

**ironworker:** (noun) a person who constructs buildings and other large structures by moving and welding together large metal beams.

**journeyman:** (noun) a person considered skilled at their trade after completing an apprenticeship.

**lay out:** (verb) in welding, to arrange on a sheet of metal the different shapes that will be cut out and put together to build an item.

**machining:** (noun) the process of making a finished part by cutting, drilling, grinding, and shaping metal using machine tools.

**motivated:** (adjective) having a strong interest in doing something.

**pipeline:** (noun) a long pipe that moves oil, natural gas, etc. from one place to another, including all of the machinery and parts needed to control the flow of the oil or gas.

**Personal Protective Equipment:** (noun) clothing and other equipment used to protect a person while they weld or are in the work area.

**scholarship:** (noun) a type of financial aid that does not need to be repaid; students usually apply for a scholarship.

**site:** (noun) the specific place where something is located.

**sparks:** (noun) tiny pieces of very hot material; in the case of grinding, sparks are made of hot metal dust.

**stainless steel:** (noun) a strong metal that does not normally rust; it is used in cookware, medical equipment, tanks that store food or water, etc.

**steel:** (noun) a strong metal made from iron and carbon used in many buildings, machines, cars, etc.

**structure:** (noun) something built or constructed.

**supervisor:** (noun) the person in charge of a group of workers.

**symbol:** (noun) a design, number, letter, etc. that represents something; for example, "$" is a symbol for "dollar."

**tape measure:** (noun) a long flat strip of metal with marks to show inches or centimeters used to measure the length of an object.

**textbook:** (noun) a book used in a class to study the subject.

**trade:** (noun) an occupation that requires special physical or hands-on skills learned at a school, on the job, or other special training; examples of trades are welding and construction.

**ventilation:** (noun) a system that removes used air and replaces it with fresh air; in the welding shop, air can become dangerous to breathe because of gases or metal dust; a ventilation system replaces that air with safe, clean air.

**vision:** (noun) the ability to see, eyesight.

**weld:** 1. (verb) to join metal together using heat; 2. (noun) the welded metal joint.

**welder fabricator:** (noun) a welder who also fabricates an item, usually in the manufacturing industry.

**welding helmet:** (noun) personal protective equipment to protect the face, neck and eyes from flash burn (similar to sunburn) and sparks made during welding.

# Online bibliography

Aghajanian, Liana. "There's a Shortage of Welders. Will More Women Fill the Gap?" The Atlantic, 21 August 2018, https://www.theatlantic.com/business/archive/2018/08/theres-a-shortage-of-welders-will-more-women-fill-the-gap/567434/

"Careers in Welding," https://www.careersinwelding.com/careers-in-welding/

"Ironworkers," Occupational Outlook Handbook, https://www.bls.gov/ooh/construction-and-extraction/structural-iron-and-steel-workers.htm

"Seven incredible facts about a career in welding," https://gowelding.org/articles/facts-about-career-welding/#content

"Welders, Cutters, Solderers, and Brazers," Occupational Outlook Handbook, https://www.bls.gov/ooh/production/welders-cutters-solderers-and-brazers.htm

"Why Welding," https://www.careersinwelding.com/why-welding/

# Acknowledgments

Creating this book as a sabbatical project was a pleasure. Each step of the way, I've been thankful for the generosity of those who have contributed.

I would most like to thank everyone in the welding department of Clackamas Community College for the help and encouragement that they offered. First, John Phelps enthusiastically shared his knowledge about welding careers, training, and his love for teaching. He provided me with a list of former students who were well into their unique welding careers with stories to tell. He suggested that I take an introductory welding course to learn about welding firsthand.

In particular, I would like to thank Marlana Tizo, my introductory course instructor, and Matt "Blue" Sabin, her teaching assistant. Marlana not only taught me how to weld, but she also shared her point of view as a woman in the welding profession. As Blue helped me to work out the kinks in my welding technique, he shared a great deal of technical information.

After that, Bruce Mulligan invited me to observe his multi-level fabrication class for a term. In class, I not only learned about welding and fabricating, but I also met the second-year students and learned from them. Bruce often shared details of his diverse career as inspiration to the students. He encouraged students to plan for achieving their goals and to reach beyond expectations.

I want to thank the many students, professionals, and instructors who interviewed with me. They told me about their personal backgrounds, their choices, and their current or future endeavors. They also gave sound advice for me to share with students who are considering welding as a program of study and career path. The interviewees provided me with the most important content of this book—real-life manifestations of education and career choices. I would never have found this kind of information in other sources.

I am so grateful to my friend Grace Warren for all of her editorial help. She worked with me on organization, formatting, writing, language choice, editing, and so much more. Her professional experience has been invaluable.

More thank-yous go to my cousin, Jackie Olson, for her expertise in working with digital formatting of text and images; to my husband Lawrence Vergun for reviewing drafts and providing advice based on prior experience with publishing; and to my daughter Madeleine Vergun for reviewing drafts and designing the book cover.

Thank you, also, Amy James Neel of Oregon Tradeswomen, Inc. for insight on women in the trades; Tim Krause for techniques used in creating graded readers; and Kyle Thomas for career and academic advising information.

Finally, I appreciate the photographers who personally donated images to this project, and those who licensed their photos with Creative Commons or Pixabay for all to use.

# Photo credits

Cover muliahusein0870 (muliahusein0870, Pixabay).

3 Paul Lindsey (plindsey_dsu, Flickr), "DSCN4546," licensed under CC BY 2.0.

5 Andrea Vergun, © 2019.

8 Chris Davis (cjdavis, Flickr), "Grinding welds," licensed under CC BY-SA 2.0. Top photo. (cropped)

8 Thom Kingston, co-founder of Spidertrax Off-Road (Spidertrax, Flickr), "Rock Bug Detailed Welding of Knuckles & Custom Bolts," licensed under CC BY 2.0. Bottom photo. (cropped)

9 Lisa Runnels (Greyerbaby, Pixabay).

10 Official U.S. Navy Imagery (Official U.S. Navy Page, Flickr), "Sailor performs an underwater fillet weld in a training pool at the ROK engineering school," licensed under CC BY 2.0. Top photo.

10 Jon Kline (JonKline, Pixabay). Bottom photo.

11 Robson Machado (Robzor, Pixabay). Top photo.

11 Andrea Vergun, © 2019. Center photo.

11 Eli Duke (eliduke, Flickr), "Portland: Columbia Boulevard Wastewater Treatment Plant," licensed under CC BY-SA 2.0. Bottom photo.

12 Paul Lindsey (plindsey_dsu, Flickr), "DSCN4663," licensed under CC BY 2.0. Top photo. (cropped)

12 Jackie Olson, used with permission. Bottom photo.

15 David Lombrozo, used with permission.

18 Ralf (Waldrebell, Pixabay).

27 Andrea Vergun, © 2019.

35 Andrea Vergun, © 2019, all photos on page.

37 Anne Olson, used with permission.

41 Andrea Vergun, © 2019, all photos on page.

47 Zach Catanzareti (Zach Catanzareti Photo, Flickr), "Noah Gragson," licensed under CC BY 2.0. (cropped)

49 Kirt Edblom (Kirt Edblom, Flickr), "Welding Grade C9 3-2.5 Titanium," licensed under CC BY-SA 2.0.

51 Mike Krzeszak (Photos by Mavis, Flickr) "Steel art structure SE Portland" licensed under CC BY 2.0. (cropped)

53 Colin Preston, used with permission.

54 John Phelps, used with permission, all photos on page.

57 BriYYZ (BriYYZ, Flickr), "Sibelius-monumentti — detail," licensed under CC BY-SA 2.0. (cropped)

**Licensing details at Creative Commons**
CC BY 2.0 and CC BY-SA 2.0:
https://creativecommons.org/licenses/by/2.0/

**Licensing details at Pixabay**
Date of Last Revision: January 09, 2019
https://pixabay.com/service/terms/#license

Made in the USA
Monee, IL
11 September 2022